BUDAPEST

24 MAY 1975
LANDED

EMBASSY OF INDIA
WASHINGTON

No. 55
18 APR 1974
LANDED
JAMAICA, W.I.

IMMIGRATION OFFICER

KINGDOM OF BAHRAIN
ENTRY 42

2 7 AUG 2008

WELCOME TO
BUSINESS friendly

Emigration Clearance
Not Required.

GERMANY
Federal Republic of Germany
FOUNDED

CHIEF IMMIGRATION OFFICER
15 OCT 1974
JAMAICA

40-016-769

提出するものです。
Do not fold.
...tted to the Immigration Inspector
Japan.

VISIT PASS
MALAYSIA IMMIGRATION
KUALA LU...

EMBASSY
OF THE UNITED
OF AMERICA

MALA

STATES
of AMERICA

A MAGYAR NÉPKÖZTÁRSASÁG
ÉRVÉNES
EGYSZERI
KÉTSZERI
TÖBBSZÖRI

gültig bis
Saalnitz, den

CERTAINLY, TRAVEL IS MORE THAN THE
SEEING OF SIGHTS; IT IS A CHANGE THAT
GOES ON, DEEP AND PERMANENT,
IN THE IDEAS OF LIVING.
– MIRIAM BEARD

HYDERABAD
24 MAY 1975
LANDED
EMBASSY
KUALA LUMPUR
19 JAN 1973
Permitted to remain until
subject to conditions below.
Consulado General
KINGDOM OF BAHRAIN
ENTRY 42
27 AUG 2008
WELCOME TO
BUSINESS
friendly
Valid for travel to
ALL COUNTRIES
Except Union of South Africa
Colony of Rhodesia
MEXICO
LANDED
JAMAICA
Not Required.
GERMANY
Republic of Germany • Federal Republic of Germany
Bundesrepublik Deutschland
FOUNDED
0478
PB5230B9
gültig bis
11 6 70
(321)
8 OCT 1978
1976
IMMIGRATION OFFICER
BUDAPEST

TO AWAKEN QUITE ALONE IN A STRANGE
TOWN IS ONE OF THE PLEASANTEST
SENSATIONS IN THE WORLD.
– FREYA STARK

...WE LEAN FORWARD TO THE NEXT CRAZY
VENTURE BENEATH THE SKIES.
– JACK KEROUAC

UNITED STATES of AMERICA
E PLURIBUS UNUM
15OCT1974
Emigration Clearance
Not Required.
Do not fold.
type or print.
is to be submitted to the Immigration Inspector
your departure from Japan.
18 APR 1974
VISIT PASS
MALAYSIA IMMIGRATION
KUALA LUMPUR
19 JAN 1973
subject to conditions below.
REF:
JAMAICA
REGIONAL PASSPORT & EMIGRATION OFFICE
GOVT. OF INDIA
HYDERABAD
EMBASSY OF THE UNITED STATES OF AMERICA
Consulado General de la Republica Dominicana Miami, Florida
DEC 2
20 MAY 1978
KINGDOM OF BAHRAIN
ENTRY 42
1976
gültig bis
Republic of Germany
IMMIGRATION CAYMAN ISLANDS
OCT 12 1996

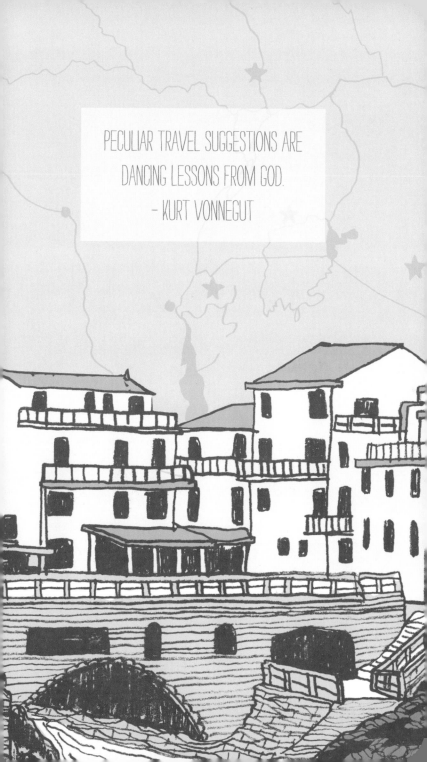

PECULIAR TRAVEL SUGGESTIONS ARE
DANCING LESSONS FROM GOD.
- KURT VONNEGUT

GOVERNMENT OF INDIA
HYDERABAD
VISIT PASS
MALAYSIA IMMIGRATION
KUALA LUMPUR
19 JAN 1973
EMBASSY OF THE UNITED STATES OF AMERICA
remain until
subject to conditions below.
REF:
15 OCT 1974
JAMAICA
Consulado General de la Republica Dominicana Miami, Florida
DEC 2
IMMIGRATION
20 MAY 1978
LANDED
JAMAICA W.I.
KINGDOM OF BAHRAIN
ENTRY 42
27 AUG 2008
WELCOME TO
BUSINESS
friendly
PASSPORT & EMIGRATION OFFICE
GOVERNMENT OF INDIA
Valid for travel to
ALL COUNTRIES
Except Union of South Africa
Colony of
Clearance
ired.
GERMANY
Federal Republic of Germany
Republic of Germany
FOUNDED 1949
Bundesrepublik Deutschland
MEXICO
0478
PR5230889
BUDAPEST
IMMIGRATION OFFICER
MALTA
DEPAR
Zinnwald · Hirschberg
Marienborn · Frankfurt (O)

I WAS BORN LOST AND TAKE
NO PLEASURE IN BEING FOUND...
- JOHN STEINBECK

EMBASSY OF INDIA
WASHINGTON

REGIONAL PASSPORT
GOVERNMENT OF
INDIA
HYDERABAD

24 MAY 1975
LANDED
JAMAICA

BUDAPEST

KINGDOM OF BAHRAIN
ENTRY 42

2 7 AUG 2008
WELCOME TO
BUSINESS
friendly

No. 55
18 APR 1974
LANDED
JAMAICA, W.I.

Emigration Clearance
Not Required.

CHIEF IMMIGRATION
15 OCT 1974
JAMAICA

40-016-769

GERMANY
FOUNDED
Bundesrepublik Deutschland

提出するものです
Do not fold.
...tted to the Immigration Inspector
Japan.

VISIT PASS
MALAYSIA IMMIGRATION
KUALA LUMPUR

ONCE IN A WHILE IT REALLY HITS
PEOPLE THAT THEY DON'T HAVE TO
EXPERIENCE THE WORLD IN THE
WAY THEY HAVE BEEN TOLD TO.
– ALAN KEIGHTLEY

HALF THE FUN OF TRAVEL IS THE
AESTHETIC OF LOSTNESS.
– RAY BRADBURY

- Consulado General
- OCT 1978
- LANDED
- MAICA
- KINGDOM OF BAHRAIN
- ENTRY 42
- 2 7 AUG 2008
- WELCOME TO
- BUSINESS friendly
- MEXICO
- Valid for Travel to
- ALL COUNTRIES
- Except Union of South Africa
- Colony of Rhodesia
- Federal Republic of Germany
- GERMANY
- FOUNDED 1992
- Bundesrepublik Deutschland
- 0478
- POST PAID
- BUDAPEST
- DNK
- 09
- PR523089
- Diesel – Zimmwald
- Elmsdorf – Marienberg – Frankfurt (O)
- Hinchberg – Pomell
- gültig bis
- 15. Juli 19
- 11. 6. 70
- 1976
- Sabnia den
- 21996
- IMMIGRATION OFFICER
- (321)
- – 8 OCT 1928
- HEATHROW
- IMMIGRATION OFFICER
- (321)
- – OCT 1928
- Dirección General de Migración
- DEC 24 2003
- UNITED STATES of AMERICA
- 150CT19

THE END IS NOTHING; THE ROAD IS ALL.
- WILLA CATHER